NORMAL WOMEN in MEDICINE

Contents

Written by Philippa Gregory

Illustrated by Monica Auriemma

Collins

1 Medicine or magic?

I bet you think that women who made potions in the "olden days" were witches on broomsticks?

Think again! They were the first doctors in British history!

Meet Matilda le Leche, a woman doctor in Berkshire in the 1200s. Matilda knew that many of the plants she grew in her garden could heal and help her patients.

She knew that honey would clean a wound, and she treated headaches with rose, lavender or sage. Patients with stomach pains drank mint tea and lemon balm. Broken bones were healed by the herb comfrey.

Matilda le Leche was so successful that she earned a lot of money and became a respected member of her town – and she was not the only woman doctor. Thousands of women were healers, doctors, surgeons, dentists, chemists and midwives in medieval England – but almost all of them have vanished from history books.

Can you be a doctor when you don't know about bodies?

X-ray machines and scanners hadn't been invented in medieval England, so doctors couldn't see bones or organs inside their patients' bodies. They didn't know that the heart moves blood around the body, or how people breathe. Worst of all, they didn't know about germs, so they had no idea what causes illness. But men interested in medicine published what they thought anyway!

Men doctors saw their own bodies as the standard. Because women's bodies are different, they were seen as strange or ill.

These famous doctors didn't really know how the body worked – but they published books anyway!

The Church also taught that women were emotional, too weepy, or too chatty and that womens' brains were too feeble to study or learn. When the first universities opened in the 1200s, they were only open to men. The universities taught the ancient Greek theory that blood and **bile** in the body made people Hot or Cold, Wet or Dry, and that disease came from being out of balance. This was wrong!

Meanwhile, women, who could not read the Latin books anyway, were nursing and healing their children, families and neighbours using the herbs, flowers and cures learnt from their mothers. Some of these worked, some did nothing – and some were harmful! But it was the best there was at the time.

This story begins almost 1,000 years ago. Women have always been healers, experimenting with cures. Women worked in medicine even when they were locked out of education, banned from working and blamed for the illnesses they were trying to heal.

This book is about all of these women.

2 Women in medicine squeezed out

In 1066, William the Conqueror invaded England and changed everything, especially for women.

1066–1600s

1066

William the Conqueror invades England – lots of surgery is needed for battle wounds.

1200s

The universities of Oxford and Cambridge are opened for men only.

1348–1349

The Black Death kills so many people that they lose their trust in healers.

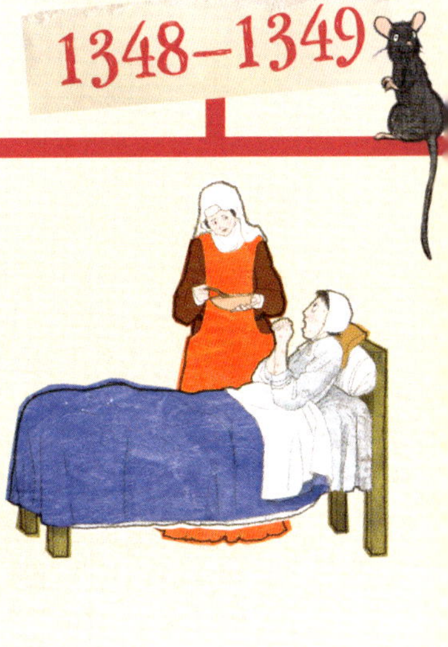

Medicine, herbalism, nursing, tooth-drawing, midwifery, bone setting, blood-letting and laying out of the dead were once the work of women. But when men-only universities opened, they ignored the knowledge of women healers.

1518–1530s

King Henry VIII closes the monasteries and abbeys where women healers learned and worked and opens a royal medical college – for men only.

1542

The first English laws are brought in against witchcraft.

1600s

Witch-hunts accuse women healers of being witches.

Apothecaries

Women specialised in gardening, farming and gathering crops in the country villages so they knew the plants that could heal. Large houses and castles had a "still room" where plants were processed for medicines. The women kept recipes of medicines that worked well and handed them down to their daughters.

These herbal remedies were written at St Augustine's Abbey in Canterbury in the 1070s.

In towns, some women had so many customers that they opened shops selling medicines.

Early hospitals

Hospitals were set up in **monasteries**, **nunneries** and **abbeys** for local patients and visitors. Talented nuns could work as doctors, nurses, surgeons, scientists and managers.

Abbess Euphemia

Euphemia was not only a nun, she was also a hospital manager, builder and garden designer! Euphemia was chosen by her fellow nuns to lead Wherwell Abbey in 1226. She added a **sanctuary**, a new hospital, toilets with running water and proper drains as well as living space for her growing team. She built the hospital away from the main buildings to prevent the spread of disease, placing it beside a river for clean water and air. She designed a **meditation** garden, grew herbs for medicines, and built a mill to grind flour. Her patients recovered better, and she became known as a pioneer of modern hospital design.

Doctors and surgeons

In the Middle Ages, barbers didn't just cut hair. They also used their razors for operations: cutting off wounded or diseased legs or arms and stitching up wounds. They pulled out bad teeth and set broken bones. It wasn't just men who were allowed to be barbers! Women could join the barber-surgeon **guilds** and train as surgeons until the 1700s.

Women could train as doctors, by serving an apprenticeship and then work as physicians. One woman called Agnes Medica was working in Huntingdonshire in 1271, and a woman called "Katherine, La Surgeon" worked in London in 1286 with her father and brother. Cecilia of Oxford was paid a daily wage to be "surgeon" for Queen Philippa, the wife of Edward III.

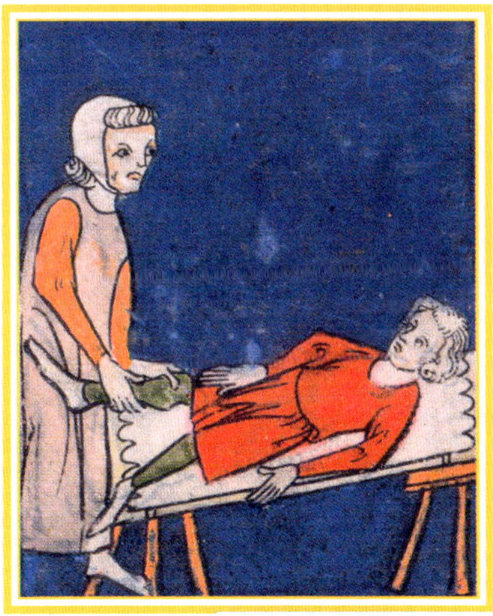

bone setting in the 1300s

Nurses and midwives

Childbirth was dangerous for mother and baby. They were helped by "midwives" – an old Anglo-Saxon word that means "wise woman". Midwives would go to a woman's house, for days or even weeks before she was due to give birth, and live with her in her bedroom. All men – even the baby's father – had to stay away.

Midwives and nurses charged very small fees for their work. In time, all the low-paid jobs in nursing were left to poor women. The most dangerous jobs, such as nursing patients with the plague and preparing dead patients for burial, were always done by poor women who couldn't afford to refuse to work.

Wise women

Every village had its own "wise woman"– a woman who was working as a midwife, healer and herbalist all in one. Sometimes they also worked as "cunning" women. Cunning women and cunning men were hired by everyone, from the lords in the castle to the poorest peasant, to defend them from curses and bad luck, to find missing objects or to make potions. Sometimes, the cunning women were skilful, sometimes they were clever, sometimes they were making it all up.

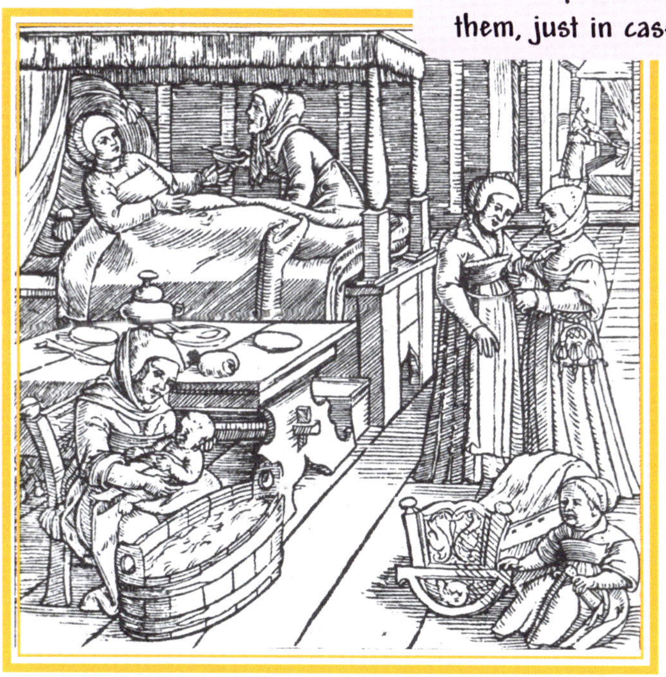

women attending a birth in the 1500s

The Black Death

In 1348, a terrible illness arrived in England from Europe. The Black Death killed as many as one in four people in some villages. There were so many deaths that people lost their faith in doctors, nurses and priests.

People turned against healers who had sold medicines, charms and spells that failed to save patients from a painful death.

Licensed doctors

Doctors, surgeons and apothecaries began to form guilds to license people for work in medicine. They ruled that only university-trained people would be given a licence – which meant only men!

Rich patients were persuaded that licensed men doctors were better than experienced women healers and that women were dangerous. But poor patients could not pay the high fees. So women healers took care of the poor and dirty – for less pay.

By the 1500s, there were changes in religion that made people anxious. The Church taught that the recurring plagues, illness and hardship were caused by a terrible sin – witchcraft. Women healers were accused of going against God's will, using magic and being witches.

POPULAR ERROURS
OR THE
Errours of the people in
matter of Physick.
Infirmum Corpus Medico
Committe fideli

Sorcery and witchcraft

New laws in the 1500s were passed against "sorcery" and "witchcraft".

People started to panic and suspect their local healer of witchcraft, especially if she was a poor old woman living alone.

She might wear old clothes, like a tall pointy hat (which was now out of fashion), have a pet and sweep her house with a battered old broom.

Over time, people thought this was what a witch looked like, and many poor old women fitted that image.

Witch-hunting lasted for 200 years! In England and Scotland, almost 90% of the accused were women and perhaps as many as 2,000 were executed.

And still good women doctors went to work!

Even during these dangerous times, women doctors carried on their work. There were women surgeons at the newly formed St Thomas' Hospital in London. Elizabeth Hall was on call at St Bartholomew's Hospital in London in the 1550s. Elizabeth Fysher used spices to make her own medicines to cure Thomas Bedforde of Coventry of a very "great swelling". Catherine Studley of Aldgate Street, London, was paid ten times the usual rate by Henry VIII to nurse his **ward** Thomas Philpot back to life in her house.

Mother Edwin worked as a surgeon at Christ's Hospital, London, in 1563; Mrs Cock was the surgeon-apothecary there in 1576, and Alice Gordon was surgeon apothecary there in 1598. Cecily Baldrye got her surgery licence from the Bishop of Norwich in 1568. Isabel Warwike was allowed to practise as a surgeon in York in 1572 because she was so well known. A midwife in Southampton was even rewarded for her work with mothers and babies in 1601. But the actual reward – called the **freedom of the city** – was given to her husband!

Lady Anne Fanshawe kept a recipe book in the 1600s and recommended a plant called cochlearia for the illness scurvy. She was right! Scurvy is caused by lack of vitamin C, and the plant is rich in the vitamin.

Lady Anne Fanshawe

3 Women push back

In 1649, the people won the Civil War against King Charles I, beheaded the king and elected a parliament instead.

1600–1800

Men doctors get into the profitable childbirth business.

1660s

William Harvey discovers how blood travels around the body.

1628

A new invention, the microscope, leads to the discovery of cells.

1665

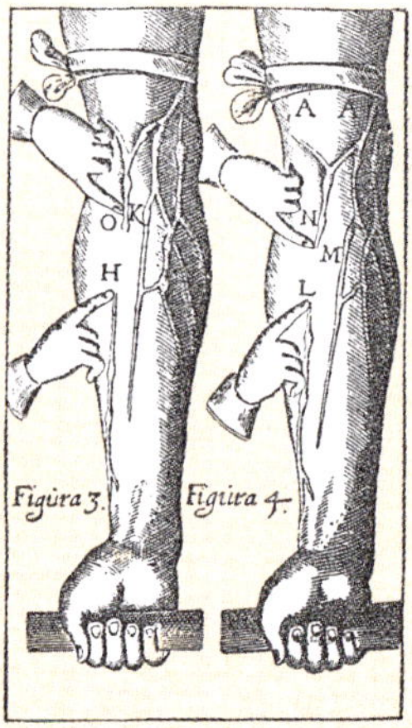

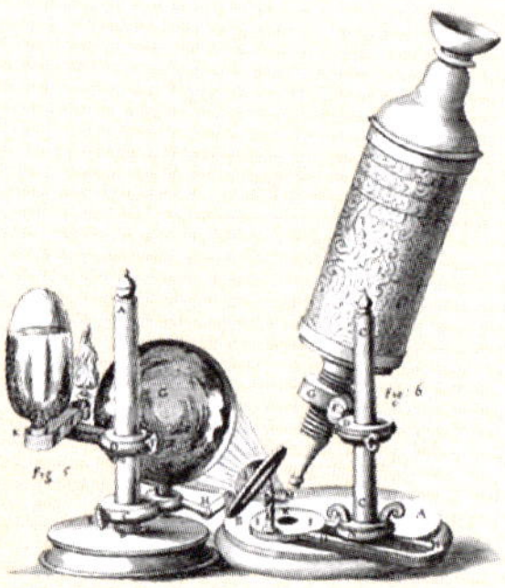

Prince Charles, the king's son, came back to England in 1660 and was crowned king. He encouraged scientific thinking – but only for men!

Despite their education at university, the men knew no more than women about the causes or cures of illness. Another great plague swept through the country in 1665, killing about 20% of the population of London.

Large hospitals open, but doctors don't understand germs and still refuse to wash their hands!

Fewer jobs in the country force poor women into towns with cramped and dirty housing.

1730s

1790s

Midwives

The greatest danger to women's lives was during the birth of their babies. In the 1600s, men doctors started to enter the birth rooms, pushing women doctors out.

The Chamberlen family of men-midwives invented forceps, life-saving tools similar to tongs, used to deliver stuck babies, but they kept the design secret for more than 100 years. They swore patients to secrecy and charged huge fees.

Poor women could not afford the rates of licensed men doctors, and so women midwives worked for poor patients while men midwives took on all the royal and noble births.

Elizabeth Cellier was a midwife and a writer of the 1600s, who argued for a college of midwives so that women could form a midwives' guild, train and license themselves. She was arrested twice and made to stand in the **pillory**.

Epidemics

No woman – rich or poor – was safe from illnesses, as busy men doctors went from one patient to another without sterilising their equipment, changing their gowns or even washing their hands. Thousands of women died.

In 1795, a naval surgeon called Alexander Gordon noticed a pattern in healthy mothers who caught a terrible fever. He realised it was the surgeons, doctors and midwives who were spreading the infection.

The wealthy men doctors ignored Alexander. One doctor said: "**Doctors are gentlemen, and gentlemen's hands are clean.**" They refused to wash their hands and women continued to die.

Inoculation

In 1715, Lady Mary Wortley Montagu was struck down with a dangerous disease called smallpox. She survived, but her brother died. She moved to Istanbul in Turkey and discovered the local people were protected against smallpox by deliberately catching a mild version of the illness (from pus or scabs).

Lady Montagu wrote to her friends in London about the method and she was so determined to prevent smallpox she ordered a surgeon to **inoculate** her young children in the same way.

Lady Montagu with one of her childrer

Word soon spread and London doctors were given a royal licence to perform trials. Dairymaids knew that catching a less dangerous virus called cowpox from their cows also gave them natural immunity from smallpox. This knowledge paved the way for vaccinations.

4 The discovery of germs and women's brains!

In the 1800s, new factories made Great Britain a rich country and forced working women into low-paid, dangerous work.

1800–1930

1832 – Kitty Wilkinson understands that disease is spread in dirt.

1800s – Rich women are diagnosed with **hysteria**.

1860 – Florence Nightingale opens a school for nurses.

At the same time, rich women were taught to do less work, be more "ladylike" and stay indoors.

Men doctors said ladies were shy and weak and needed to rest. Ladies were so bored they became ill ... and were told they needed even MORE rest to recover.

Louis Pasteur discovers germs.

1862

Three women open a school for doctors.

1874

Formal training for midwives is launched.

1902

Germs

During an epidemic in 1832, Kitty Wilkinson, a poor woman with a little laundry business in Liverpool, let neighbours disinfect clothes in her washtub for a penny a week. She wasn't a doctor, but Kitty believed that washing hands and boiling clothes prevented the spread of illness.

Kitty became known as the "saint of the slums", for saving many lives. She argued for public bathhouses so that people without bathrooms could wash. When the first one opened in 1842, Kitty became superintendent and was honoured by Queen Victoria with a silver teapot.

Which is the VERY THING you need in an epidemic.

In 1854, a young doctor, John Snow, traced an outbreak of a fatal disease called cholera to one single water pump in Soho, London. Many families got their drinking water from it.

John Snow

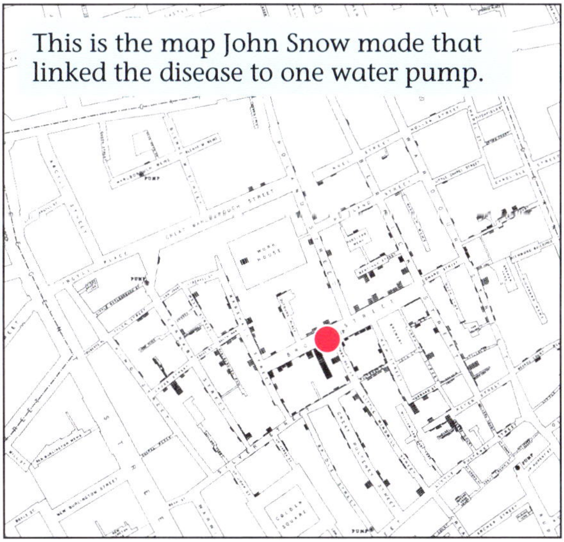

This is the map John Snow made that linked the disease to one water pump.

Sewage and pollution had **contaminated** the water, and the people who drank from the pump got sick, then passed on the germs to others.

About 100,000 people died in Britain in three cholera outbreaks in the 1800s.

You can still see the water pump today.

Nobody knew how illness passed from one person to another until 1861, when Louis Pasteur and Joseph Lister proved that disease was caused by germs. After that, people started to use medicines called antiseptics to kill germs, and the government built drains to keep sewage contained, and pipes to bring clean water to people's homes.

The Lady with the Lamp

Florence Nightingale is famous for the work she did in the Crimean War in 1853. There is a well-known picture of her as the "lady with the lamp", walking around a hospital in the dark, caring for the soldiers as they slept. But her greatest work was as a mathematician and scientist, reviewing data to improve care in hospitals.

Florence discovered that more men were dying in the war hospitals from illness than from battle wounds. She reduced deaths by improving the drains, making sure that hospital wards had good air and that everyone washed their hands.

Florence Nightingale was very influential in her career, and created a programme of training for nurses, but women were still not allowed to be doctors! Men doctors still believed that women's brains were not strong enough to study anything.

Mary Seacole

Mary Seacole was working in Crimea at the same time as Florence Nightingale. She travelled there herself and built her own boarding house to support wounded soldiers. She didn't have any help from the government or from Florence Nightingale, probably because she was a Black woman at a time of great racism. Despite this prejudice against her, she cared for all the soldiers and was awarded the Crimea Medal for her service.

Mary Seacole

Women doctors

Most histories of women doctors in Britain start with Elizabeth Blackwell in the 1850s, but Margaret Ann Bulkley took a new name and identity and trained as a surgeon in 1810. Under the name of James Barry, they joined the British Army and had a successful career all around the world, working on improving the conditions and health of both soldiers and local people. Dr James Barry's biological sex was only discovered at their death in 1865.

This is a difficult story for a historian to explain, as the most important part – what Dr Barry thought of themself – is not known.

Should Dr Barry be considered as a woman who pretended to be a man to get the career and life that she wanted? Or should they be considered as someone who truly lived they way they wanted to?

Dr James Barry

Elizabeth Blackwell, an English woman studying in the United States, was the first woman to get a medical degree. When she **graduated**, the head of her university bowed to her as a sign of his respect. Elizabeth Blackwell made several trips home to England and was the first woman to have her name registered as a qualified British doctor in 1859.

Elizabeth Blackwell

But she couldn't practise in the UK as the law was quickly changed to stop women who had qualified abroad from seeing patients.

Dr Blackwell practised in the United States and supported other women, including Elizabeth Garrett Anderson, who became the second British woman doctor.

Elizabeth Garrett Anderson loved learning and complained that her school didn't offer Maths or Science to girls. After finishing school, she worked as a nurse in the operating theatre at Middlesex Hospital, but she was not allowed to enrol at the hospital's medical school. Instead, she took lessons with the hospital's apothecary and was allowed to observe classes and some lectures. After studying privately, she applied to the Society of Apothecaries. They tried to stop her taking a place, but she eventually got her doctor's licence from them in 1865. The Society of Apothecaries quickly changed their rules to stop any more women joining.

Elizabeth Garrett Anderson

Sophia Jex-Blake worked as a Maths tutor, but was determined to become a doctor. In 1869, she applied to study Medicine at the University of Edinburgh, but they would not change their rules to allow one woman to join. So, Sophia advertised for other women and five other women stepped up. Together, they forced the University of Edinburgh to give them places. The male students bullied them and a crowd of 200 male students threw litter and mud at them when they arrived to take their final exam. Even though all the women passed, the university refused to give them their degrees!

AN APPEAL

For **LADIES** who may wish to join
Ms. SOPHIA JEX-BLAKE on a truly
BRAVE and **HISTORIC ENDEAVOUR:**

To enter **MEDICAL COURSES** at the
UNIVERSITY OF EDINBURGH.

As supported by ***The Scotsman*** Newspaper.

Sophia continued campaigning, and she established the London School of Medicine for Women with Elizabeth Garrett Anderson and Elizabeth Blackwell. Eventually, in 1876, the law was changed to license any qualified doctors – even women – and Sophia passed exams in Germany and Ireland to become the third woman doctor in the UK.

Sophia Jex-Blake

Call the midwife!

Despite the success of women doctors, midwives were still campaigning for recognition and training. In 1902, there was a breakthrough when the government created a qualification for midwives for women who had the time and money to study, but some women healers, who had been delivering babies safely for years, did not and they were not allowed to register or call themselves qualified midwives. More and more patients were persuaded to go to hospital to give birth and not stay at home with experienced, but unqualified, helpers.

The First World War

As most men doctors went to war in the First World War (1914–1918), hospitals and clinics back in Britain had to employ women in their place. Around 1,000 women worked as doctors and they were called "lady doctors".

Even today, people sometimes say "woman doctor" but they never say "man doctor", as if the very word "doctor" means "man"!

The First Aid Nursing Yeomanry (FANY) was founded in 1907 and was open only to wealthy women who owned their own horse! Unlike nurses, the FANY saw themselves as paramedics on horseback, rescuing the wounded and giving first aid. When war broke out, a FANY unit travelled to France with an ambulance – but the British Army would not use them. So, they worked for the Belgian Army instead, driving ambulances, opening a hospital and nursing wounded soldiers. Halfway through the war, the British government changed its mind and asked the women for help!

Toupie Lowther

Toupie was an extraordinary woman. She was a motorist, fencer, weightlifter, jujitsu champion and international tennis player. She took her own team of 30 women drivers and 20 ambulances to France. The British Army would not use her all-women ambulances, so they served the French Army instead.

The number of women doctors doubled by the 1920s, but after the war the men doctors came home, and several medical schools banned women – again! This time they said there were too many doctors, and that women would waste their medical training by marrying and giving up doctoring. Some medical schools were still open to women applicants, but they cut the number of places. At St Mary's in London, in 1925, the male students complained and said the attendance of women was creating "bad feeling" and was ruining the school's reputation for rugby and athletics.

What you *really* want from a medical school is good rugby players!

5 Women squeeze in

By the 1940s, women were working in all aspects of medicine. When the Second World War started, there was an increased demand for women in medicine, but still some medical schools refused to train women.

1940–present

1945

Women are persuaded back into home life after taking on many jobs, including working in hospitals and ambulances, during the war.

1948

The National Health Service is founded. Women are employed in hospitals and clinics (often doing low-paid and unskilled work).

1953

Scientist Rosalind Franklin discovers the structure of **DNA** but is paid less than the men in her team.

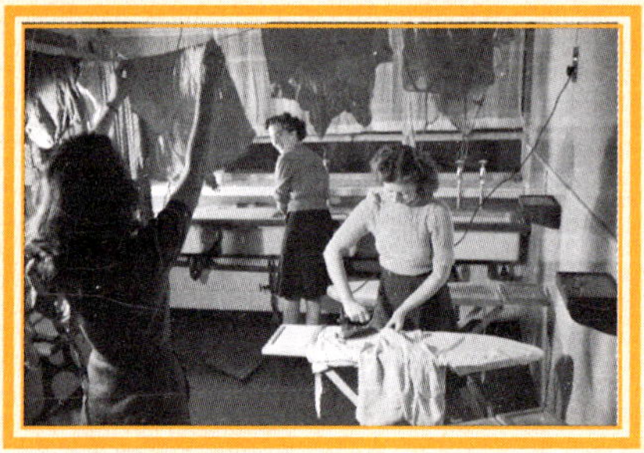

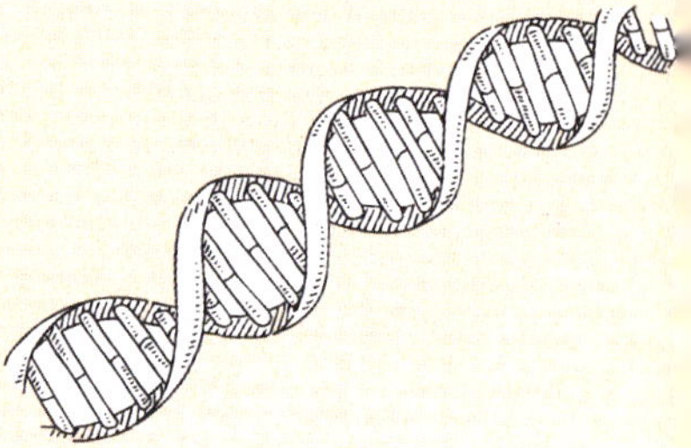

In 1944, medical schools that wanted government funding had to accept a "reasonable proportion" of women.

That sounds great, but a "reasonable proportion" was only 20% – a fifth of all the students!

About 20% of doctors are women.

New laws against unfairness force medical schools to take women as well as men and pay them the same.

For the first time ever, there are more licensed women doctors than men.

1965

1975

2025

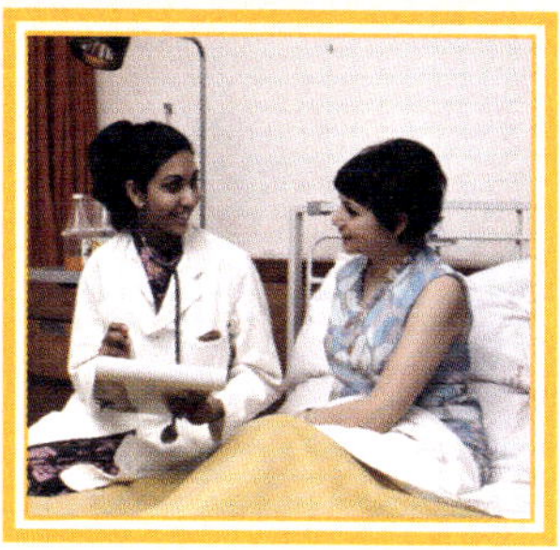

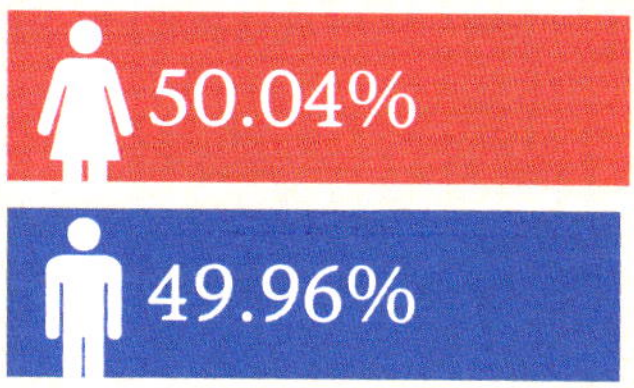

The National Health Service

The National Health Service was formed in 1948 to provide free healthcare to everyone. It's not clear how many women worked in the NHS in its first years, but there were fewer women than men and they were mostly in lower-paid, part-time roles.

Equality – not quite!

During the 1950s, women were told they should stay at home to look after children and not work at all. Some industries banned women from working after marriage.

By 1965, women made up nearly 21% of all doctors on the medical register.

Even in the mid-1970s, most medical schools put a limit on women students: no more than one third.

In 1975, new laws said men and women must be treated equally and paid the same rate for the same work.

This sounds great – and some jobs were paid equally. But other workplaces managed to wriggle out of the law. They continued to treat women unfairly and pay them less than men.

Elizabeth Nneka Anionwu

Elizabeth left school when she was 16 and worked as a school nurse assistant. She became very interested in sickle-cell disease, which was so rare that she had to go to the United States to study it.

In 1979, she came home to England and opened the first sickle-cell centre in Brent to treat patients with sickle-cell cancer. There are now more than 30 centres like this in the UK – all based on Elizabeth Anionwu's first centre.

Elizabeth was inspired by other female nurses in history. She wrote a biography of Mary Seacole and unveiled a statue of her in 2016 at St Thomas' Hospital.

Medicine today

When women get a fair chance, they take it! There are now more women than men getting into medical school because they have better grades. In 2025 – for the first time ever – there were more licensed women doctors than men.

Women are not only working in medicine as doctors and nurses, they are working as scientists and inventors.

Sarah Catherine Gilbert

Sarah was working at Oxford University on vaccines against flu when she read one of the first reports of a new sort of flu that was spreading quickly. It was COVID-19 and became the worst **pandemic** in a century. Sarah Gilbert started to research COVID-19, and in just two weeks she had discovered a vaccine against the deadly virus. When her vaccine was approved for use in the UK, more than three billion doses were also supplied to countries worldwide, saving millions of lives.

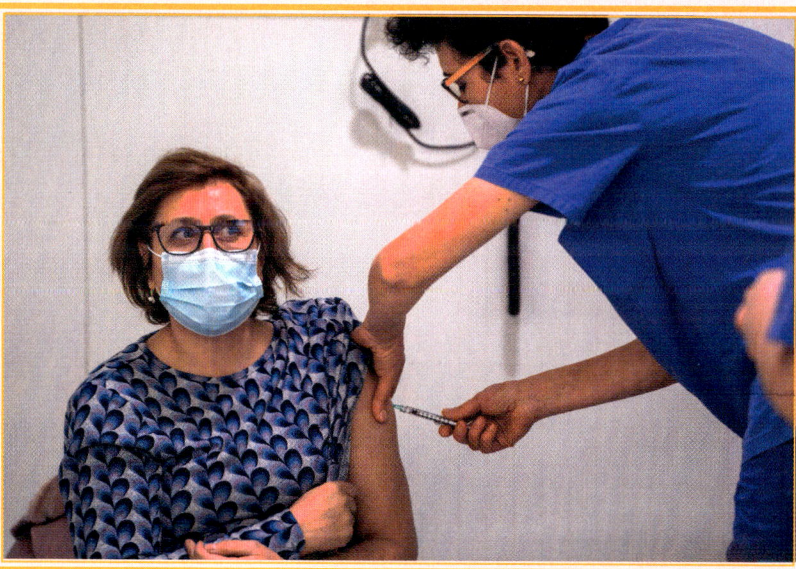

Making a difference

The history of women in medicine shows us that women, even in the distant past, were always capable of working alongside men as equals.

But when women are told that they can't do something – that they are NATURALLY unable to study – some accept the limits on their lives and some become ill or unhappy. This isn't good for men either – it puts a lot of pressure on them. But some women go on trying, and some succeed.

Professor Dame Sally Davies was the first woman to be England's Chief Medical Officer.

Reshma Saujani founded Girls Who Code, an organisation which aims to empower women in science.

Throughout history, many women have ignored the people who said they couldn't work in medicine. They have carried on working, studying and qualifying. These are the women who won medical careers and made a path that others have followed.

The women in this book show that believing in yourself really can make a difference.

Patricia Bath invented the Laserphaco Probe to better treat cataracts, helping to restore vision for millions around the world.

Dame Sue Hill is the Chief Scientific Officer for the NHS and leads a team of 50,000 research scientists.

Glossary

abbeys	buildings where monks or nuns live
bile	liquid produced in your body by your liver
contaminated	made dirty by the addition of harmful substances
DNA	found inside the human body, DNA carries all the information about how we look and function and is unique to each person
freedom of the city	the right to work, trade and join a guild in a city that you don't live in
graduated	completed studies and received an award
guilds	organisations for people with the same trade
hysteria	a state of uncontrolled emotions
inoculate	to inject a patient with a weak form of a disease to prevent them getting the disease
meditation	a practice of being calm and silent
monasteries	buildings where monks live together
nunneries	buildings where nuns live together
pandemic	when a disease affects people over a very wide area

pillory	a wooden frame with holes for the head and hands, which is used as a punishment
sanctuary	a safe place
sewage	waste matter from homes and factories
ward	someone, usually a child, who is cared for by a guardian

Index

A timeline of women in medicine

1200–1300s

Every village had its own "wise woman"– a woman who was working as a midwife, healer and herbalist all in one.

1348–1349

The Black Death killed so many people that they lost their trust in healers.

1600s

Witch-hunts accused women healers of being witches.

1700s

Large hospitals opened, but doctors didn't understand germs and still refused to wash their hands!

1832

Kitty Wilkinson understood that disease is spread in dirt.

1860

Florence Nightingale opened a school for nurses.

1876

The law was changed to license any qualified doctors – even women.

1939–1945

Women worked in hospitals and ambulances during the war.

1975

New laws against unfairness forced medical schools to take women as well as men and pay them the same.

2025

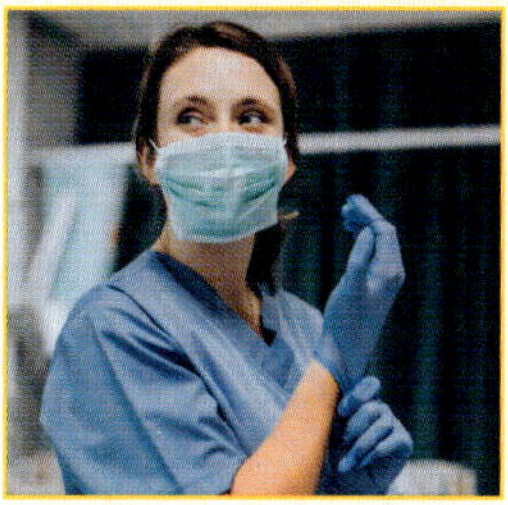

For the first time ever, there were more licensed women doctors than men.

Ideas for reading

Written by Gill Matthews
Primary Literacy Consultant

Reading objectives:

- retrieve, record and present information from non-fiction
- draw inferences and justify inferences with evidence
- summarise the main ideas drawn from more than one paragraph, identifying key details that support the main ideas

Spoken language objectives:

- listen and respond appropriately to adults and their peers
- participate in discussions, presentations, performances, role play, improvisations and debates
- consider and evaluate different viewpoints, attending to and building on the contributions of others

Curriculum links: Science: PSHE: physical health and mental wellbeing; History: changes in an aspect of social history; Science: animals including humans

Interest words: qualified, recognition, breakthrough

Resources: individual whiteboards or paper

Build a context for reading

- Look at the front cover and read the blurb together. Explain that this is a historical non-fiction book that looks at the history of women in medicine.
- Discuss the term 'medicine' and invite children to name roles they know of within the world of medicine.

Understand and apply reading strategies

- Open the book at the contents page and invite children to read the chapter titles. Point out the dates in the titles and discuss how this book is written in chronological order, from 1066 until the present day. Consider together why the book may have been written in this way, and the benefits of reading a history book in date order.
- Turn to the glossary at the back of the book and discuss any unfamiliar words and their definitions. Remind children to look out for these words when they appear in bold in the book.